The Economics
of Revolution

D0317498

The Economics of Revolution

The Economics
of Revolution
By David DeGraw

The Economics of Revolution

The Economics of Revolution
Published by David DeGraw
New York, NY

ISBN 978-1-312-53041-6

September 17, 2014
First edition print

Cover art by Shepard Fairey

Contact: David@DavidDeGraw.org
www.DavidDeGraw.org

Declaration of Independence ~

"When in the Course of human events, it becomes necessary for one people to dissolve the political bands which have connected them with another... a decent respect to the opinions of mankind requires that they should *declare the causes which impel them to the separation.*"

The Economics of Revolution

CONTENTS

PART I

PEAK INEQUALITY: THE .01% AND THE IMPOVERISHMENT OF SOCIETY

PART II

TRANSCEND CONDITIONED CONSCIOUSNESS

PART III

NOW IS THE TIME

The Economics of Revolution

PART I

PEAK INEQUALITY: THE .01% AND THE IMPOVERISHMENT OF SOCIETY

An extensive analysis of economic conditions and government policy reveals that the need for *significant systemic change* is now a *mathematical fact*. Corruption, greed and economic inequality have reached a peak tipping point. Due to the consolidation of wealth, the majority of the population cannot generate enough income to keep up with the cost of living. In the present economy, under current government policy, 70% of the population is now sentenced to an impoverished existence.

Let's take an in-depth look at the evidence.

Chapter 1
The Ultra-Rich .01%

*"There is no such thing as the liberty or effective power
of an individual, group, or class, except in relation to
the liberties, the effective powers, of other individuals,
groups or classes."*
~ John Dewey, Liberty & Social Control

To see how corrupt the United States government has become,
just *follow the money*. According to the most recent Federal
Reserve *Flow of Funds* report, US households currently have an
all-time high $82 trillion in overall wealth. If that wealth were
spread out evenly, every US household would now have $712k.
However, as of the end of 2013, the median household only had
$56k in wealth. From 2007 - 2013, overall wealth increased 26%,
while the median household lost a shocking 43% of their wealth.
If median wealth continues to decline at this rate, over 50% of US
households will be bankrupt within the next decade.

The fact that the majority of households are losing so much
wealth in a time of record-breaking overall wealth demonstrates
how systemically corrupt the economy has become. To begin to
grasp the scale of corruption, let's analyze how much wealth has
been consolidated within the economic top 1% of the population.

The latest comprehensive look at wealth distribution data reveals
that the "ultra-rich" economic top 0.01% of US households now
has an all-time high 11.1% of overall wealth. The next tier, the
99.9% – 99.99% has 10.4%, and the top 99% – 99.9% has 18.3%.
In total, the top 1% now has an all-time high 39.8% of wealth.

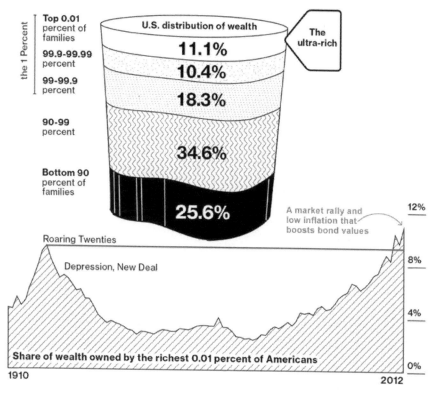

U.S. distribution of wealth

the 1 Percent

Top 0.01 percent of families — **11.1%**

99.9-99.99 percent — **10.4%**

99-99.9 percent — **18.3%**

90-99 percent — **34.6%**

Bottom 90 percent of families — **25.6%**

The ultra-rich

A market rally and low inflation that boosts bond values

12%

8%

4%

Roaring Twenties

Depression, New Deal

Share of wealth owned by the richest 0.01 percent of Americans

0%

1910   2012

GRAPHIC ADAPTED FROM BLOOMBERG BUSINESSWEEK. DATA: SAEZ, ZUCMAN 2014

When we correlate wealth distribution percentages with the $82 trillion in overall wealth reported by the Federal Reserve, it reveals that the top .01% has a stunning $9.1 trillion in wealth. In total, the top 1% has a mind-blowing $32.6 trillion.

To begin to comprehend wealth of this magnitude, one trillion is equal to 1000 billion. $32.6 trillion written out is $32,600,000,000,000.00.

Having that much wealth consolidated within a mere 1% of the population, while a record number of people toil in poverty and debt, is a *crime against humanity*. For example, it would only cost 0.5% of the 1%'s wealth to *eliminate poverty nationwide*. Also consider that at least 40% of the 1%'s *accounted* for wealth is *sitting idle*. That's an astonishing $13 trillion in wealth hoarded away, *unused*.

Once you truly understand how much $32.6 trillion is, and realize how just a fraction of that wealth could dramatically evolve society for the benefit of all, the argument for *significant systemic change* is solid. However, as scandalous as these statistics are, they do not factor in trillions of dollars more in *unaccounted for offshore wealth*, which makes the overall situation sound significantly better than it actually is and hides the true depth of the crisis from popular consciousness. (We will analyze hidden wealth in Chapter 4.)

Looking toward the future, current trends reveal that the rate in which inequality is growing is increasing rapidly. Overall wealth increased by $1.5 trillion in the first quarter of 2014. If wealth keeps increasing at the current rate, there will be an increase of $6 trillion in 2014. How will this wealth be distributed? If you look at income gains since 2009, 95% of them have gone to the top 1%.

We Are the 99.99%

There are now many people within the top 1% who are much closer in wealth to the middle class than they are the ultra-rich. Greed has grown so extreme that even within the top 1% inequality is soaring. The top 1% of the 1%, the .01%, now has 28% of the 1%'s wealth. When you factor in hidden wealth, they have an estimated 33% of the 1%'s wealth. An individual must have over $100 million in wealth to be in the .01%.

In 1980, the richest .01% was already consolidating wealth at a systemically unhealthy rate. Since then, they have more than quadrupled their share of overall wealth. Meanwhile, households who fall between the top 10% and the top 0.1% have actually been losing their share of overall wealth.

As the ultra-rich .01% amasses unprecedented wealth, they are forcing the overwhelming majority of the population into *extreme economic insecurity* and *ever-increasing debt*.

Chapter 2
The Systematic Impoverishment of Society

"The war against working people should be understood to be a real war. Specifically in the US, which happens to have a highly class-conscious business class. They have long seen themselves as fighting a bitter class war, except they don't want anybody else to know about it."
~ Noam Chomsky, Propaganda & Control of the American Mind

If you are struggling to get by and running up debt to make ends meet, it is not your fault. It is the intentional outcome of government policy and economic central planning. In the present economy, it is *impossible* for 70% of the working age population to earn enough income to afford *basic necessities* without taking on *ever-increasing* levels of debt, which they will *never* be able to pay back because there are not enough jobs that generate the necessary income to keep up with the cost of living.

For every 3.4 working age people, there is only one that can generate an income high enough to cover the cost of living without taking on debt. In total, only 20% of the overall population currently generates enough income to sustain the cost of living. As a result, poverty and declining living standards are much more prevalent throughout US society than the government and corporate media report. Let's take a look at the reality behind mainstream propaganda...

The US Government & Statistical Fraud

The government engages in outright *statistical fraud* on the most often cited economic indicators, from the unemployment rate to poverty and inflation rates. Even the use of the Gross Domestic Product measurement as an indicator for overall economic health is incredibly deceptive.

The mainstream media not only incessantly repeats these bogus measurements, they drastically underreport the growing epidemic of poverty. According to a study by Fairness and Accuracy in Reporting, "on average, someone affected by poverty appeared on any nightly news show only once every 20 days.... An average of just 2.7 seconds per 22-minute nightly news program was devoted to segments where poverty was mentioned."

On the rare occasion when poverty is actually mentioned, the government's Census Bureau poverty rate of 15% may be cited. When it comes to the overall employment situation, you will hear the Bureau of Labor Statistics' unemployment rate, which is presently hovering around 6%. While these statistics are alarming, they drastically undercount the severity of the present crisis. Those two statistics are pure propaganda and mask the economic suffering of *over 222 million US citizens*.

Before analyzing the employment situation, let's look at how the government calculates the poverty rate. The methodology behind the federal poverty rate was designed in 1963. It is *incredibly* outdated and *significantly undercounts* how much it costs to live in today's economy. It uses the extremely flawed Consumer Price Index (CPI) inflation rate to establish the poverty threshold. Many vital economic statistics that the government reports are based on this *fraudulent* inflation rate.

To give a more positive impression of overall economic health, the government has "revised" the methodology behind the CPI rate over 20 times since 1970. The CPI currently has inflation rising at a 2% annual rate. If inflation was calculated the way it was in 1980, the current rate would be 10%. When you take a deeper look into how this difference impacts vital economic statistics, it reveals a *much different* picture of the US economy.

Cost of Living

While the government claims a 2% annual inflation rate, the actual cost of living has been skyrocketing. Here's the reality of the situation...

The US now has the most expensive healthcare system in the world. There has been a 22% increase in out-of-pocket hospital expenses over the past year. In the first quarter of 2014, healthcare spending rose at the fastest pace in 10 years. The cost of giving birth has tripled since 1996, childbirth out-of-pocket expenses increased fourfold from 2004 to 2010. The cost of childcare increased by 70% from 1985 to 2011. From 1994 to May 2014, the cost of childcare has been more than double the CPI inflation rate.

The overall cost of raising a child has risen 40% in the past decade, *not counting the cost of college.* Since 1986, the cost of college tuition has increased by 498 percent, compared to the 117% CPI inflation rate over that timeframe. Student loan debt has increased threefold over the last decade. The amount of money students are borrowing to pay tuition bills doubled from 2005 to 2012.

Looking at basic food costs, from 2002 to 2012, total CPI inflation was 28%. Consider the following price increases over that timeframe: Eggs 73%, Ground Beef 61%, Turkey 56%, White Bread 39%, Spaghetti & Macaroni 44%, Peanut Butter 40%, Coffee 90%, Orange Juice 46%, Apples 43%, Margarine 143%.

This dramatic rise in the basic cost of living, the amount of money that people need to survive, which is all but ignored by the CPI in the federal poverty threshold calculation, only reveals part of the government's deception on poverty. Beyond the fraudulent inflation measurement, the Census Bureau does not adequately account for the differences in cost of living based on geographic locations. For instance, the cost of living in large population states like New York and California, as compared to the costs in more rural lower population Southern and Midwestern states.

When you realistically account for *real* inflation and geographically based cost of living, how much does it cost to cover basic necessities?

The Economic Policy Institute (EPI) has the most comprehensive look at the costs of living and how much money a family needs to cover basic necessities based on the city they live in. The EPI accounts for the costs of housing, food, healthcare, childcare, transportation and taxes. *They do not factor in the costs of a college education or retirement.*

Based on EPI calculations, a *family of four* needs to make $63,364 a year to cover basic necessities. Compare that to the government's Census Bureau calculation using the CPI inflation rate and non-geographic accounting, which puts this threshold for a *family of four* at a mere $23,600.

In relation to the government's poverty rate, the Economic Policy Institute's numbers sound extremely high. However, they use very modest costs. For example, they use Topeka, Kansas as their median family budget area and calculate the cost of housing for a *family of four* at only $692 a month. When you analyze geographically based costs, you can see how expensive it is for a family to live in larger population cities:

- New York HUD Metro FMR Area: $94,676
- Los Angeles-Long Beach: $74,605
- Chicago-Naperville-Joliet: $73,055
- Philadelphia-Camden-Wilmington: $77,928

- Washington, DC: $89,643
- San Francisco: $82,639
- Phoenix: $68,742
- San Diego-Carlsbad-San Marcos: $71,673
- San Jose-Sunnyvale-Santa Clara: $77,619

To give more context, USA Today recently analyzed how much *moderate* costs of living for a family of four are today. They calculated that the average family needs to generate an annual income of $130k. Their estimate was more than double the median EPI cost of $63k, primarily because they factored in the costs of owning a home, one car, retirement and education.

Now, consider that the current annual median household income is only $51k per year. While overall wealth and the cost of living have skyrocketed, median household income has declined 8.3% since 2007 and 9% since 1999. To further demonstrate how dramatically the cost of living has truly risen since 2007, while median household income declined 8.3%, their overall wealth declined 43%.

For more historical context and to further demonstrate how corrupt the government and economic system have become; if household income had kept pace with the overall economy since 1970, the current annual median would be $95k, almost double what it presently is. On top of that, it was normal to have only one wage-earner per household in 1970, as compared to two now.

Extreme Poverty

If we look at the government poverty threshold for what it truly is, an indicator of *extreme* poverty, then it has a little more legitimacy. As the National Center for Children in Poverty reported on the government's poverty threshold, "Research shows that, on average, families need an income of about twice that level to cover basic expenses."

When we count the percentage of the population at double the government's poverty threshold as living in poverty, the poverty rate explodes from 15% of the population to 47%. Now you can see one of the reasons why the government falsifies the inflation rate. The government will not make this *long overdue adjustment* because that would mean they have to admit that *150 million people* are currently living in poverty and simply cannot afford the cost of basic necessities.

According to the Census Bureau, 28% of children are now *born* into poverty. This marks a dramatic increase from an already alarming 25% in 2008. In total, the Census Bureau reports that 22% of children live in poverty. However, when we make the proper adjustments to the methodology of the poverty rate, an even more horrifying 45% of children live in poverty. That means there are currently 33,389,063 US children living in households that *cannot afford basic necessities.*

It would take only 0.3% of the 1%'s wealth to lift every one of these children out of poverty.

Overall, from 2000 to 2010 the Census Bureau found that the percentage of people living in poverty-stricken neighborhoods grew from 18.1% to 25.7%. Extrapolating out to today, we can estimate that 82 million people presently live in *extreme* poverty-stricken neighborhoods.

Extreme poverty-stricken neighborhoods can become a relic of the past with 0.5% of the 1%'s wealth.

For a deeper understanding of why poverty is growing so rapidly while overall wealth is also growing, let's analyze the government's fraudulent unemployment statistics.

Unemployment & Underemployment

Other than the deceptive poverty rate, unemployment is much worse than the 6% that the government reports. The 6% rate does not include part-time workers who need full-time work, long-term unemployed people who have not been able to find work for over six months, and "discouraged workers" who do not consistently look for work. When you account for those groups, as the Bureau of Labor Statistics (BLS) did until 1994, the real unemployment rate is currently 23.2%.

For an example of how deceptive government unemployment reporting is, the BLS June 2014 jobs report decreased the unemployment rate and was portrayed in the mainstream media as a very positive result with 288k jobs added. However, in June, 523k full-time jobs were *eliminated*, and 800k part-time jobs were added, providing the *illusion of job growth* and a reduction in the government's unemployment rate. Due to this trend, there are now over 7.5 million underemployed workers who are "part-time for economic reasons" because they have had their hours cut and/or cannot find full-time employment. *None of these people are counted in the official government unemployment total.*

Since 2007, well-paying paying jobs have become rare and low-paying full-time, part-time and temporary jobs have replaced them. This has also been a downside of the new healthcare law, as companies are cutting back full-time employment so they don't have to pay for workers' healthcare. In total, 50% of jobs created over the past three years are "low-paying," mostly in retail, food service or temporary help. Low-paying jobs pay *80% or less of median wages.*

The bottom line, in a nation of 318.6 million people, with a working age population of 213 million people, there are now only 118 million full-time jobs and 28 million part-time jobs, according to the BLS. However, also according to the BLS, there are currently only 106.6 million full-time workers. In other words, it is *impossible* for *half* of the working age population to get a full-time job. On top of that, of the current 118 million full-time jobs, 47% of them generate annual salaries below $35k per year.

Chapter 3
Economic Slavery

"We are entering a new phase in human history - one in which fewer and fewer workers will be needed to produce the goods and services for the global population."
~ Jeremy Rifkin, The End of Work

Beyond unemployment and underemployment, the percentage of full-time working poor has grown significantly. US workers are presently producing twice as much wealth per work hour than they were in 1980. Instead of median incomes doubling since then, they have stagnated. The gap between wealth production and median income is now at an all-time high.

Based on the latest available individual level income data, 40% of workers make less than full-time minimum wage workers made in 1968, roughly $20k per year according to the suppressed CPI inflation rate. More realistic adjustments for inflation will reveal a much higher total. For example, the current federal minimum wage is $7.25 an hour. If minimum wage had kept pace with overall income inflation since 1968, the minimum wage would now be $21.16, which means a full-time minimum wage worker would now be making $44k a year. However, the *median* annual wage is now only $27,519. Based on income inflation, only 22% of the working age population and 15% of the overall population currently have an annual income higher than a full-time minimum wage worker had in 1968.

The average person needs to generate $35k in annual income to cover the cost of basic necessities. Looking at the actual spending habits of the average worker, you need to generate an income of $42k to cover annual expenses. If we use $35k as our threshold for a living wage, only 30% of the working age population and 20% of the overall population generate an annual income over $35k. For every 3.4 working age people, there is one that generates an income high enough to cover the cost of basic necessities without taking on debt.

Keep in mind, that does *not* factor in the cost of paying off student debt. Average student debt is presently $29,400. If paid off over a 10-year period, at an average 4.6% interest rate, it costs $306 per month, $3672 annually. In this situation, a person needs to make an annual income of $38,672 to cover the cost of living plus their student debt. Only 27% of the working age population and 18% of the overall population generate that much income. For every 3.7 working age people, there is one that can sustain the cost of basic necessities *plus* the average student loan debt *without taking on more debt*.

Therefore, in the current economy, 73% of people with student debt will not be able to pay it back while also maintaining the cost of living, without going *deeper into debt*. The US government has sentenced you to a lifetime of *ever-increasing* debt and *ever-declining* living standards.

Mathematically Eliminated from the American Dream

For a worker to cover their own cost of living and the cost of *one* child, they will need to make roughly $45k a year. Only 22% of the working age population and 15% of the overall population currently generate enough income to support one child. For every one person that can generate enough income to sustain the cost of basic necessities for themselves and one child, there are 4.5 working age people.

Now, think back to the American dream that prevailed from the 1950s – 70s. Each family had *one* wage-earner supporting three children and one other adult who would care for the children.

While this was considered the "American dream," it is also the basis of a healthy society.

How healthy is our society and how many people can afford to live the American dream in today's economy?

With today's cost of living, just to cover basic necessities it will cost $80k per year to pull this off in the median family area, Topeka, Kansas. In the current economy, only 5.8% of the population can currently generate enough income to live the traditional American dream in Topeka. Clearly, we are not in Kansas anymore.

Levittown, New York was the first suburb that gave birth to the American dream. Try pulling off the American dream in its birthplace and it will cost $125k a year. Only 2% of the population can pull that off.

Once again, *these baseline costs do not* take college or retirement costs into account. With the reduced costs in childcare, due to one person in the family focused on taking care of the children, they can at least put some money away for college, as long as they don't go away for vacation and none of their children go to a *private* school.

Beyond these baseline costs, looking at *moderate* costs for a *family of four* owning a home in a median family area, with one car, education and retirement costs factored in, it will cost $130k a year. Add a third child and a second car into the mix and it will cost roughly $150k a year. Only 1.46% of the overall population makes over $150k per year. In other words, in the current economy, the *average* traditional American Dream is only attainable for the 1%. The 99% has been mathematically eliminated from the traditional American Dream. If they want to have a family and own a home, they are now sentenced to a lifetime of economic insecurity and *ever-increasing debt*.

As for retirement, if you American dreamers think you are going to retire at 65, it's time to wake up.

There Is No Escaping Debt

According to the National Institute on Retirement Security, "the median amount a family nearing retirement has saved for their post-work lives is $12,000." As 76 million Baby Boomers are due to retire, the real toll of this economic crisis is going to hit home in a huge way.

Up until now, Social Security has been the savior. Currently 57 million people receive Social Security benefits. In the present economy, that works out to two full-time workers for every one person collecting benefits. Adding 76 million to the 57 million people currently drawing benefits would mean 133 million retirees to 118 full-time jobs. Even factoring in death rates, with new full-time jobs a rarity in today's economy, having one retired person to one full-time worker will soon be a reality.

In fact, Social Security is already giving out more money than it is taking in. From 2010 – 2012, there was a $150 billion deficit. However, the Social Security trust fund is supposed to have a $2.7 trillion in surplus. In reality, all that money was already spent on wars, bailouts and tax cuts for the rich. As Charles Hugh Smith explains, "when Social Security runs a deficit, the Treasury funds it by selling Treasury bonds, the same way it funds any other deficit spending. If the Treasury can't sell bonds, the phantom nature of the Trust Fund will be revealed."

Given the corruption in Washington and the current fiscal debate, the likelihood of Social Security maintaining it promised returns is minimal. On top of that, the dramatic rise in healthcare costs and decline in full-time jobs make the current system inadequate and unsustainable. According to the Census Bureau, 54% of people over age 64 would be living in poverty without Social Security.

The probability that the more fortunate members of the Baby Boom generation will collect full pensions and be able to sell off their assets to cover the cost of basic necessities in this economy is also highly problematic. In "The Happy Story of Boomers Retiring on Their Generational Wealth Is Wrong," Charles Hugh Smith sums up the situation:

> "[Boomers'] wealth will shrivel once they start selling assets en masse. The reality is neither Gen-X nor Gen-Y have the savings, income or desire to buy bubble-level assets from their elders. This reality has been papered over for the past 5 years of super-low interest rates, which have enabled unqualified buyers to buy overpriced assets with modest income. Once the defaults start pouring in (and/or interest rates rise), the reality will become visible: you can't cash in your wealth if there are no buyers.

> There are numerous other fatal flaws with the happy story that 76 million Boomers can retire on full pensions and live off their home equity and stock portfolios.... Pension funds based on annual returns of 7.5% will be unable to fund the promised pensions when annual returns decline to negative 5%. As John Hussman has explained, every asset bubble in effect siphons off all the future return: when the bubble finally pops, average annual returns are subpar or negative for years."

Another Wave of Foreclosures on the Horizon

Since 2007, over 5.5 million families have lost their homes to foreclosure. The impact of that is horrifying to think about. The decision to bailout the banks to the extent that they were able to give out all-time record salaries and bonuses to the very people who caused the crisis, while millions of American families were thrown out of their homes is the epitome of tyranny and corruption.

Unfortunately, the foreclosure crisis is far from over. Six million families are still underwater on their mortgages, and this number will increase. Their average negative equity is a shocking 33%. As Ellen Brown recently summed it up, "40% of mortgages nationally are either underwater or nearly so, meaning more is owed on the home than it is worth. Seventy percent of homes that are deeply underwater wind up in default. Worse, second mortgages are due for a reset. Over the next several years, principal payments will be added to interest-only payments on second mortgages taken out during the boom years. Many borrowers will be unable to afford the higher payments. The anticipated result is another disastrous wave of foreclosures."

Looking at the overall picture, mortgage debt-to-wages is *more than double* the historic average. To make matters even worse, the Federal Reserve has been fraudulently inflating housing prices. As part of their wealth extraction operation they currently own $1.7 trillion in Mortgage-backed securities and $2.4 trillion in Treasury securities. (We will take a look into how the Federal Reserve benefits the economic top .01% at the determent of everyone else in Chapter 4.)

The Illusion of Prosperity & A Tsunami of Debt

The inevitable insolvency of the overwhelming majority of the population hasn't hit home yet because they have taken on ever-increasing levels of debt to maintain the *illusion of prosperity*. Other than the staggering national debt that the corrupted government has run up, US citizens have now taken on $12 trillion in personal debt.

On average, that's $50k of debt for every US citizen over the age of 17. Again, it cannot be stated enough, in the current economy under present government policy, it is *impossible* for this debt to be paid off while maintaining the cost of basic necessities. Therefore, overall debt will continue to skyrocket. Even if interest rates on these debts dropped to 0%, as the Federal

Reserve has done for a select few of their friends on Wall Street, there is no way for people to earn enough income to keep up with cost of living, let alone pay back their debts. On top of that, the already usurious interest rates on these debts are increasing. In fact, the spark that set off the global financial crisis in the first place is heating up once again:

> "During the first quarter [of 2014], 3.7 million credit cards were issued to subprime borrowers, up a head-scratching 39% from a year earlier, and the most since 2008. A third of all cards issued were subprime, also the most since 2008.... In the first quarter, the average [interest] rate was 21.1%, up from 20.2% a year ago, while prime borrowers paid an average of 12.9% on their credit cards, and while banks that are lending them the money paid nearly 0%."

If current trends continue and current policies remain in place, 90% of the US population is heading for insolvency. That may sound like an exaggeration that is too absurd to be true. However, as the Guardian recently reported in an article headlined, "The Coming Debt Tsunami:"

> "So why look down the road – say, to 2017 – and worry? Here's why: because the debt held by American households is rising ominously. And unless our economic policies change, that debt balloon, powered by radical income inequality, is going to become the next bust....
>
> Falling government deficits are being replaced by rising debts on everyone else's ledgers.... the majority of Americans – the 90% – will once again do what was done before: borrow, and then borrow more. By early 2017... it should be apparent that we're reliving an alarming history. Middle- and low-income households have been following a trajectory of an ever-higher ratio of debt to income....
>
> The evidence demonstrates that the de-leveraging of the very rich and the indebtedness of almost everyone else move in tandem; they follow the same trend line. In short, there's a

strong and continuous correlation between the rich getting richer, and the poor – make that the 90% – going deeper into debt.... The more – proportionally – that the top 10% has prospered, saved and invested (naturally, the gains found their way into the financial markets), the more the bottom 90% has borrowed....

Insolvency for the 90% has become... 'the new normal'. Unsustainable? Of course.... Under the current disastrous economic and tax policies, we can look forward to rapid increases in debt for both corporations and households from at least 2015 to 2017: a tsunami of debt."

The first wave of the coming tsunami of debt has already begun to wash ashore. For the first time since the depth of the recession, credit card debt is now rising faster than wage growth, yet another ominous indicator of what's to come.

Crimes Against Humanity

Behind all of the statistics presented in this report is immense physical and psychological trauma. The stress of economic insecurity compounds the problem by leading to health problems, which dramatically increase costs of living. Economic insecurity drives people to expensive healthcare, medications, drug use and crime. Beyond the moral and humanitarian imperative, recent studies prove that the cost of poverty to overall society is far higher than the cost of *eliminating poverty*.

The shortsighted greed of the .01% is causing the unnecessary suffering of an unprecedented number of people. Their consolidation of wealth has created a system of *economic slavery*. In a wealthy and technologically advanced society, it is a *crime against humanity* for a majority of the population to be toiling in extreme debt, poverty, unemployment and low-wage jobs.

Chapter 4
Hidden Wealth
& Shadow Banking

"This new report focuses our attention on a huge 'black hole' in the world economy that has never before been measured – private offshore wealth, and the vast amounts of untaxed income that it produces.... Using the most comprehensive data set ever assembled, we have been able to triangulate on the size and growth of this black hole." ~ Tax Justice Network, The Price of Offshore Revisited

The evidence presented in this report thus far makes a very solid *mathematical* case for *significant systemic change*. However, to get a more complete understanding of how corrupt the global economic system is, we also need to factor in wealth that is hidden from public view. Disregarding trillions of dollars in hidden wealth just because the wealthy have the ability to *illegally* hide it is an absolute injustice. It is completely ignoring a critical aspect of what is now the *greatest theft of wealth in human history*.

Hidden wealth estimates vary widely. Many of them only take a partial look at the most basic methods of offshoring wealth. Given the unprecedented growth of wealth over the past generation, the secretive methods used to hide it have evolved far beyond well-known tax havens in Switzerland and small-island jurisdictions such as the Bahamas. While estimates based on banking secrecy and tax havens help to give us a more accurate picture of overall wealth, they do not give a total view.

Research by Gabriel Zucman, which analyzed banking secrecy, estimated that "around 8% of the global financial wealth of households is held in tax havens." If we correlate this 8% with the $82 trillion in *accounted for* wealth reported by the Federal Reserve, that would be an additional $6.6 trillion for the wealthy, bringing the richest 1% up to roughly $39 trillion in overall wealth.

However, to get a more complete understanding of the reality of the situation, the most wide-ranging look into hidden wealth was done in 2012 by economist John Henry in partnership with the Tax Justice Network (TJN). They estimated that there was $21-$32 trillion hidden globally at the end of 2010. As shocking as that sounds, that estimate *still* did not give a complete view of hidden wealth. As they put it, "We consider these numbers to be conservative. This is only financial wealth and excludes a welter of real estate, yachts and other nonfinancial assets owned via offshore structures."

We also need to consider that overall US household wealth is up 30% and has increased by $25 trillion since the end of 2010. Globally, High Net Worth Individual investible wealth has increased 19% since then, and has begun to accelerate at a record pace. In 2013, it increased globally by 14%, with a 17% increase in North America, which is now at an all-time high. Given these factors, and several others that will be explained below, the higher TJN estimation of $32 trillion in 2012 *is* conservative today.

Correlating TJN's wealth estimates with US distribution percentages is not an exact science but it gives a *much more accurate* total of overall wealth than excluding it. Based on TJN's estimation, Ultra High Net Worth Individuals (UHNWI) accounted for 48% of hidden wealth. If we correlate that to the overall estimate of $32 trillion, it equates to $15.4 trillion for the UHNWI population. The US accounts for 35% of the UHNWI population, which correlates to $5.4 trillion. In the next tier, High Net Worth Individuals (HNWI) also accounted for 48% of hidden wealth.

The US currently has 42% of the HNWI population, which correlates to $6.5 trillion. The additional 4% of hidden wealth is estimated to be held below the economic top 1% of the US population, which correlates to roughly $538 billion.

This brings the estimated total of hidden US wealth to $12.4 trillion, with $11.9 trillion of that held within the top 1%. We can now estimate that the top .01% has $14.5 trillion in wealth, the top .1% has $26.4 trillion and in total the top 1% has $44.5 trillion.

Percentile	% of household wealth	Accounted For	Hidden	Total wealth	% of household wealth
0.01%	11.10%	$9.1	$5.4	$14.5	15.4%
99.9 - 99.99%	10.40%	$8.5	$3.4	$11.9	12.6%
99% - 99.9%	18.30%	$15.0	$3.1	$18.1	19.2%
Top 1%	**39.8%**	**$32.6**	**$11.9**	**$44.5**	**47.1%**
90-99%	34.6%	$28.4	$0.5	$28.9	30.6%
Bottom 90%	25.6%	$21.0	$0.0	$21.0	22.2%
	100.0%	$82.0	$12.4	**$94.4**	100.0%
	Total households	115,226,802			
	Avg wealth per household	$711,640			
	Avg household plus offshore	$819,254			
	2013 Median Household	$56,335			

After we factor in estimated hidden wealth, the top 1%'s share of overall wealth increases from 39.8% to 47.1%. To glimpse the scale of theft, if hidden wealth were spread out evenly over every US household, that would be an extra $108k per household, increasing average household wealth to $819k. That is approximately 15 times greater than the 2013 median household with only $56k in wealth. Also consider that the estimated $12.4 trillion that the wealthy have *stashed* away is roughly equivalent to the $12 trillion in total household debt.

On top of the *unaccounted for* $12 trillion in hidden wealth that the 1% has, they have $13 trillion in *accounted for* wealth that is also sitting in bank deposits. Therefore, they have a total of *$25 trillion in unused wealth*. That is enough to give $217k to every US household.

After revealing the 1%'s $32.6 trillion in *accounted for* wealth, estimating that they have another $11.9 trillion in hidden wealth may seem like an unnecessary risk that will invite attacks to undermine the credibility of this analysis. That is an understandable reaction. However, in the grand scheme of things, that reaction is based on a dangerously naïve understanding of the global economic system. In reality, if we ever get a full look at hidden wealth, the top 1% could more realistically own 50% of overall wealth. It would not be surprising if the top 1% actually has $50 trillion in wealth, with $18 trillion of that held by the .01%.

Hopefully, government apologists, establishment economists, mainstream pundits and well-paid public relations experts will attack these numbers. Public awareness of *hidden wealth* and the total amount of *accounted for* wealth that the ultra-rich have is an urgent priority. Debate over these numbers will further highlight the *absurdly corrupt and scandalous nature of the entire system.*

Here's how TJN summed up the situation:

> "Despite taking pains to err on the conservative side, the results are astonishing. First, this hidden offshore sector is large enough to make a significant difference to all of our conventional measures of inequality. Since most of missing financial wealth belongs to a tiny elite, the impact is staggering.
>
> For most countries, global financial inequality is not only much greater than we suspected, but it has been growing much faster.... it turns out that this offshore sector – which specializes in tax dodging is basically designed and operated, not by shady no name banks located in sultry islands, but by the world's largest private banks, law firms, and accounting firms, headquartered in First World capitals like London, New York, and Geneva.
>
> Our detailed analysis of these banks shows that the leaders are the very same ones that have figured so prominently in government bailouts and other recent financial chicanery.... it is scandalous that official institutions like the Bank for International Settlements, the IMF, the World Bank, the OECD, and the G20, as well as leading central banks, have devoted so

little research to this sector. This scandal is made worse by the fact that they already have much of the data needed to estimate this sector more carefully."

The bottom line, there is overwhelming evidence proving that the Federal Reserve, global central banking system and the US government are a front for the ultra-rich. In short, we know that the biggest players on Wall Street engaged in trillions of dollars in fraudulent activity and the Federal Reserve created trillions of dollars out of thin air, mostly in secrecy, to cover it up and continue the looting of wealth. Instead of holding people accountable, the US government bailed them out.

The stock market is now a blatantly rigged *wealth extraction operation*. To name just a few of the more well known rigging operations; high frequency trading, dark pools, Quantitative Easing (QE) and the Zero Interest Rate Policy (ZIRP), which gives interest free money to a select handful of "primary dealers" on Wall Street. All of these highly corrupt schemes enrich the .01% at the expense of the overwhelming majority of the population.

Quantitative Easing

To get a deeper understanding of an aspect of the wealth extraction operation, let's take a closer look at the Federal Reserve's Quantitative Easing (QE) program. Through QE, the Federal Reserve created $4 trillion, out of thin air, under the guise of stimulating job growth. However, since 2007 the economy has lost 14.4 million full-time workers, and the population has grown by 17 million people. Most of the $4 trillion created through QE went into the pockets of the richest .01% of the population. In reality, QE is a massive welfare program for the mega-wealthy. With that $4 trillion, the Federal Reserve could have *completely eliminated unemployment and poverty*.

Clearly, giving another $4 trillion to people who already had $21 trillion in *unused* wealth was not an effective stimulus for the overall economy. If they truly wanted to stimulate the economy, they could have given the $4 trillion to every non-millionaire household, which would have been $40,000 per household, or they could have given 114,285,714 people $35,000 each. If we clawback QE from the ultra-rich, we can eliminate poverty nationwide and guarantee a *Living Income* to every person over the age of 18.

Shadow Banking

Another major aspect of the wealth extraction operation that the *public is not allowed to see*, which also makes the $12.4 trillion in hidden wealth a *conservative* estimate, is the shadow banking system. The .01% participates in a secret *unregulated* derivatives market that is worth an estimated $2010 trillion in notional value. The global financial crisis was a result of this secret market, which features credit default swaps. The truth is, the public and the government have *no idea* what is happening within this market, and neither do economists who try to reveal how much wealth the .01% truly has. Look behind the curtain of the Federal Reserve and shadow banking system and the true neo-feudal nature of the global economy is revealed in spectacular fashion.

A public understanding of how much wealth the ultra-rich truly have will create a critical mass of people who are aware that the global economy and US government have *zero* legitimacy. The essential elements that keep this scam going are the extensive propaganda system that paid off and uninformed mainstream media pundits uphold, and a military, intelligence and police complex that *protects the perpetrators of the greatest theft of wealth in human history*. As far as the corrupt government is concerned, the theft of trillions is too big to reveal. If the people have to suffer as a consequence, so be it.

The emperor has no clothes. He's standing right in front of you, with *$50 trillion* in wealth, as you go deeper into debt and toil in economic insecurity.

Chapter 5

The Aristocracy &
The Death of Liberty

"The first truth is that the liberty of a democracy is not safe if the people tolerate the growth of private power to a point where it becomes stronger than their democratic State itself. That, in its essence, is fascism – ownership of government by an individual, by a group or by any other controlling private power."
~ Franklin D. Roosevelt

From the "monied aristocracy" to the "Gilded Age" and the "Roaring 20s," extreme wealth inequality has always threatened freedom and democracy. Many of the most respected US presidents have highlighted the fight against concentrated wealth as the first priority of a free society. Even in times of war, presidents have referred to bankers as being a bigger threat to the country than enemies on the battlefield.

Visionaries and leaders such as Buckminster Fuller and President Franklin D. Roosevelt saw the modern advancement of technology and increase in productivity and wealth creation occurring. They began to envision a *near* future where people could regain their freedom from the *dreary compulsion of industrialism.* Roosevelt proposed an *Economic Bill of Rights* that would guard against unhealthy levels of inequality and guarantee *economic security for every citizen.* He equated the concentration of wealth to "fascism" and "gangster rule." Upon accepting his second nomination as president, before World War II started, Roosevelt declared a war for economic freedom *against the .01%.* He compared the wealthiest members of society to the British monarchy during revolutionary times:

> "... the average man once more confronts the problem that faced the Minute Man.... The savings of the average family, the capital of the small-businessmen, the investments set aside for old age - other people's money - these were tools which the new economic royalty used to dig itself in.... For too many of us the political equality we once had won was meaningless in the face of economic inequality.

> A small group had concentrated into their own hands an almost complete control over other people's property, other people's money, other people's labor - other people's lives.... Against economic tyranny such as this.... the collapse of 1929 showed up the despotism for what it was.... The royalists of the economic order have conceded that political freedom was the business of the government, but they have maintained that economic slavery was nobody's business....

> These economic royalists complain that we seek to overthrow the institutions of America. What they really complain of is that we seek to take away their power. Our allegiance to American institutions requires the overthrow of this kind of power. In vain they seek to hide behind the flag and the Constitution. In their blindness they forget what the flag and the Constitution stand for. Now, as always, they stand for democracy, not tyranny; for freedom, not subjection; and against a dictatorship by mob rule and the over-privileged....

> America we are waging a great and successful war. It is not alone a war against want and destitution and economic demoralization. It is more than that; it is a war for the survival of democracy.... I accept the commission you have tendered me. I join with you. I am enlisted for the duration of the war."

The war against the .01% was temporarily derailed when World War II began. However, even at the *height of WWII*, during Roosevelt's 1944 State of the Union address, he kept the focus on the .01% and said that they were "the greatest problem" facing the nation. He called out "a noisy minority" which "maintains an uproar of demands for special favors for special groups." He described them as, "pests who swarm through the lobbies of the Congress and the cocktail bars of Washington, representing these special groups as opposed to the basic interests of the Nation as a whole...."

Roosevelt saw World War II as an extension of the deeper battle against *"economic slavery,"* wealth inequality and the .01% who prevailed in the 1920s and led the nation into the Great Depression. Here's another excerpt from his 1944 State of the Union address:

> "We are united in determination that this war shall not be followed by another interim which leads to new disaster... that we shall not repeat the excesses of the wild twenties... if history were to repeat itself and we were to return to the so-called 'normalcy' of the 1920's -- then it is certain that even though we shall have conquered our enemies on the battlefields abroad, we shall have yielded to the spirit of Fascism here at home...."

When looking at the *unprecedented* level of wealth inequality in today's society, it is obvious that "the spirit of Fascism" has prevailed. Instead of increased productivity and wealth being a very good thing for overall society, the shortsighted greed of the .01% has systematically taken the increase in wealth for themselves, robbing everyone else of a life of liberty, economic security and freedom.

The "gangster rule" that Roosevelt warned against is now the norm. The .01% acts with impunity, totally above the law, engaging in *trillions of dollars in fraudulent activity* without being held accountable. In fact, they are rewarded with all-time record-breaking bonuses and *ever-increasing wealth.*

The .01% "economic royalists" hand down their dictates through centrally planned economic policy and government legislation designed to keep the population economically insecure, subservient and enslaved in debt. Through their ownership of mainstream media companies they keep the masses in ignorance, wholly unaware of the paradigm shift in technology and wealth creation that should have provided economic security and made life much more enjoyable for everyone well over a generation ago.

We now live in a neo-feudal society. The evidence is undeniable. The indentured servant is now the indebted wage slave. A recent scientific study revealed that the United States government is subservient to the whim of the .01%. Political office is now merely a stepping-stone and initiation process that politicians go through to be accepted into the aristocracy.

The .01% aristocracy is exactly what the first American Revolution was against. It was Thomas Jefferson's understanding of the aristocracy's ability to consolidate wealth and subvert government that led him to believe that *every generation required its own revolution.* Here are two prophetic quotes from Jefferson:

> "Our country is now taking so steady a course as to show by what road it will pass to destruction, to wit: by consolidation of power first, and then corruption, its necessary consequence."

> "I hope we shall take warning from the example and crush in its birth the aristocracy of our monied corporations which dare already to challenge our government to a trial of strength and bid defiance to the laws of our country."

In discussing "the spirit of the people" and the need to "nourish and perpetuate that spirit," Jefferson also said, "I am not among those who fear the people. They, and not the rich, are our dependence for continued freedom. And to preserve their independence, we must not let our rulers load us with perpetual debt. We must make our election between *economy and liberty*, or *profusion and servitude.*"

Peer passed propaganda and you will see that the aristocratic "spirit of fascism" has conquered the "spirit of the people." As wealth and power have been consolidation in unprecedented fashion, the overwhelming majority toils in "servitude" and "perpetual debt." Economic tyranny is the new normal.

The Coming Revolution

"All countries are basically social arrangements, accommodations to changing circumstances. No matter how permanent and even sacred they may seem... in fact they are all artificial and temporary."
~ Strobe Talbott

We present this report as a *declaration of the causes which impel our separation* from a corrupt and oppressive government. After analyzing current policies and economic conditions, it is now evident that the systematic exploitation of a majority of the population will continue without redress.

The need for *significant systemic change* is now a *mathematical fact.* Corruption, greed and economic inequality have reached a peak tipping point. As more people grow aware of the deliberate systemic nature of their unnecessary suffering, exploitation and oppression, there will soon be a critical mass who will insist upon nothing less than absolute revolution. The delusional political class and mainstream media uphold the status quo as if it is insurmountable. In reality, it is highly unstable, unsustainable and collapsing at an increasing rate.

"The civilization may still seem brilliant because it possesses an outward front, the work of a long past, but is in reality an edifice crumbling to ruin... destined to fall in at the first storm."
~ Gustave Le Bon, The Crowd

Revolution is inevitable.

The Economics of Revolution

PART II

TRANSCEND CONDITIONED CONSCIOUSNESS

Becoming aware of the $94.4 trillion in overall wealth, and how just a fraction of that wealth can be used to evolve society for the benefit of all, opens up and expands our consciousness. Now, we will analyze the system of propaganda that conditions and contracts mass consciousness to understand how the .01% gets away with consolidating so much wealth and power.

"The wise man said, 'The people of your culture are the captives of a story.'

I sat there blinking for a while. 'I know of no such story,' I told him at last.

'You mean you've never heard of it?'

'That's right.'

The wise man nodded. 'That's because there's no *need* to hear of it. There's no need to name it or discuss it. Every one of you knows it by heart by the time you're six or seven. And you hear it incessantly, because every medium of education pours it out incessantly. It's like the humming of a distant motor that never stops, it becomes a sound that's no longer heard at all.'

'This is very interesting,' I told him. 'But it's also a little hard to believe.'

The wise man's eyes closed gently in an indulgent smile. 'Belief is not required. Once you know this story, you'll hear it everywhere in your culture, and you'll be astonished that the people around you don't hear it as well but merely take it in. They're no more aware of its functioning than they are of the functioning of gravity.'"

~ Adapted from Daniel Quinn, The Invisible Wall

Chapter 6
Conditioned Consciousness

"To subdue the enemy without fighting is the highest skill."
~ Sun Tzu, The Art of War

Even the most independent minded people vastly underestimate how mentally conditioned we all are. In 1929, in response to the growing propaganda system, John Dewey said, "We live exposed to the greatest flood of mass suggestion humanity has ever experienced." Since then, the flood of mass suggestion has grown exponentially.

For two obvious examples, let's look at television consumption and advertising. The average American watches more than five hours of TV a day, *every single day of their life*. American children view more than 40,000 ads per year, *every single year of their life*. Think about that. That's intensive mental domination administered on a daily basis, *from the cradle to the grave*.

Ultimately, as Phil Merikle summed it up, "It's what advertisers have known all along: if we just keep the exposure rate up, people will be influenced." Repetition, it's all about repetition. Repetitive messages fill our mental atmosphere. They are like the air we breathe. To paraphrase Philip Lesley in *Managing the Human Climate*, 'When a message appears all around you, you tend to accept it and take it for granted. You find yourself surrounded by it and your subconscious mind absorbs the climate of repetitive ideas.'

Repetitive messages form the origins of our thoughts. It's where our perception, desires and opinions are born. As Marshall McLuhan said, the mass media is an extension of our nervous system. The mainstream media is the software on which our thoughts run; it's our operating system. Repetitive mainstream propaganda creates a belief system, popular reference points, archetypes, mental patterns, a mindset and groupthink.

Groupthink is a *highly infectious disease*. You must be ever vigilant to escape the tyranny of groupthink and cultural conditioning. As Walter Lippmann said in *Public Opinion*, "In the great blooming, buzzing confusion of the outer world, we pick out what our culture has already defined for us, and we tend to perceive that which we have picked out in the form stereotyped for us by our culture."

To remix a quote from Dostoevsky's *Notes from Underground*, 'Leave people alone without mass media and they will be lost and confused. They will not know what to support, what to cling to, what to love and what to hate, what to respect and what to despise.' As Malcolm X summed it up, "The media is the most powerful entity on earth. They have the power to make the innocent guilty and to make the guilty innocent, and that's power. Because they control the minds of the masses."

The mainstream media creates a false reality, a "pseudo-environment." People are born and raised inside mass media created illusions. They become isolated and detached from wider reality. As Eduardo Galeano put it, "The majority must resign itself to the consumption of fantasy. Illusions of wealth are sold to the poor, illusions of freedom to the oppressed, dreams of victory to the defeated and of power to the weak."

As Harold Lasswell said in 1927, "The new antidote to willfulness is propaganda. If the mass will be free of chains of iron, it must accept its chains of silver. If it will not love, honor, and obey, it must not expect to escape seduction."

Most people live in a mental cage now, they toil on mentally conditioned plantations. As Gore Vidal put it in *The Great Unmentionable*, "We are like people born in a cage and unable to visualize any world beyond our familiar bars.... That opinion the few create in order to control the many has seen to it that we are kept in permanent ignorance of our actual estate."

To paraphrase a wise man who once fought against the .01%, 'The depravity and amount of suffering required for the accumulation of such a staggering magnitude of wealth, in the hands of a few, is kept out of the mass media, and it is not easy to make people understand this.' Especially when we have an all-encompassing propaganda system.

The Economics of Revolution

Chapter 7
Enlightened Despotism

'The propagandized masses not only do not disapprove of atrocities committed by the .01%, but they have a remarkable capacity for not even hearing about them.'
~ Adapted from George Orwell, Politics and the English Language

The most prevalent censorship today is censorship of any thoughts outside of corporate ideology. Information that leads to critical thought on the established power structure is omitted from public consciousness. Any thoughts that veer outside the spectrum of status quo supporting opinion are left out of the debate.

The mainstream press does not cover the most vital social, economic and political issues. The more important something is, the less they report on it. If mentioned at all, it's mentioned in passing, with little, if any, in-depth reporting, discussion and debate on it. *It's censorship by omission and bullshit on repetition.*

The Spectrum of Thinkable Thought

The mainstream media limits the debate within a Republican vs. Democrat parameter. If the two dominate political parties, which are both funded and controlled by the .01%, do not focus on an issue, it is omitted from public consciousness.

As Noam Chomsky observed, this is how propaganda and social control posing as freedom and democracy works: "The smart way to keep people passive and obedient is to strictly limit the spectrum of acceptable opinion, but allow very lively debate within that spectrum.... That gives people the sense that there's freethinking going on, while all the time the presuppositions of the system are being reinforced by the limits put on the range of the debate."

To paraphrase Alex Carey, the mainstream media creates 'the spectrum of thinkable thought. They set the terms of debate, to determine the kinds of questions that will dominate public consciousness, people's thoughts. They set the political agenda in ways that are favorable to corporate interests. The debate is never about the curtailment of the manipulative power of global corporations.'

Imagine how different our current economic conditions would be if the mainstream media kept discussing how a small percentage of the population has $50 trillion in wealth, then they started debating how we could use just a fraction of that wealth to solve problems, create solutions and evolve society. What if they reported the fact that 0.5% of the 1%'s wealth could eliminate poverty?

Imagine if the mainstream media focused coverage on the trillions of dollars in fraudulent activity and theft that got us into this crisis. What if they reported on the $12 trillion in hidden wealth? What if they reported the fact that 70% of the population cannot generate enough income to afford the cost of living without taking on ever-increasing debt?

What if they focused our attention on the Business Roundtable and the 147 interconnected companies that control 50% of the world's economy and dominate both political parties? What if they reported on all the wealth and resources that those corporations control, then debated how that wealth and those resources could be redeployed to get us onto a sustainable path?

These are just a few of the economic issues that real journalism would make known to the public in a genuine democracy. Pick any issue that affects overall society that you are knowledgeable about and look at how the mainstream media covers that issue, *if they even cover it at all.*

Speaking of real democracy, imagine in-depth coverage on the corruption of our political process through a system of bribery that makes the mafia look like amateurs.

What if we had real journalism instead of infotainment and talking heads reading teleprompters and reciting .01% talking points? Would the .01% get away with consolidating wealth and power in such extreme and unprecedented fashion?

Once your consciousness expands beyond the narrow parameters set by the two dominate .01% controlled political parties and the mainstream media, and you become aware of the unprecedented wealth that is available, you see how truly corrupt, shortsighted and obsolete our system is. You then realize that our mainstream media system *is pure propaganda.*

Mainstream media is the most effective weapon of mass oppression humanity has ever known. As William Blum said, "Propaganda is to democracy what violence is to dictatorships." When it comes to oppression, it's all cyclical yet evolutionary. Physical force has evolved into mental conditioning. It's "enlightened despotism."

In the land of propaganda, tyranny is democracy.

The harsh truth is that we are not freethinking participatory citizens involved in the decision-making processes that guide our lives and determine our fate. We are mentally conditioned to be spectators and servants, reactionary consumers and mindless wage slaves.

The Economics of Revolution

Chapter 8
Totalitarian Minds

"Propaganda is today a greater danger to mankind
than any of the other more grandly advertised
threats hanging over the human race..."
~ *Jacques Ellul, Propaganda*

In Jacques Ellul's 1965 analysis of the social mind, *Propaganda: The Formation of Men's Attitudes*, he summed up the present crisis with stunning insight:

"Propaganda ruins not only democratic ideas but also democratic behavior – the foundation of democracy, the very quality without which it cannot exist.... Propaganda destroys its very foundations. It creates a man who is suited to a totalitarian society....

A man who lives in a democratic society and who is subjected to propaganda is being drained of the democratic content itself – of the style of democratic life, understanding of others... he is a 'totalitarian man with democratic convictions,' but those convictions do not change his behavior in the least. Such contradiction is in no way felt by the individual for whom democracy has become a myth and a set of democratic imperatives, merely stimuli that activate conditioned reflexives.

The word democracy, having become a simple incitation, no longer has anything to do with democratic behavior. And the citizen can repeat indefinitely 'the sacred formulas of democracy' while acting like a storm trooper."

That is the most accurate description of the modern propagandized "citizen" that I've ever come across. Ellul went on to explain the inherent danger of our two-party system and the general apathy Americans have toward politics:

"The conflicting propaganda of opposing parties is essentially what leads to political abstention. But this is not the abstention of the free spirit which asserts itself; it is the result of resignation, the external symptom of a series of inhibitions. Such a man has not decided to abstain; under diverse pressures, subjected to shocks and distortions, he can no longer (even if he wanted to) perform a political act. What is even more serious is that this inhibition not only is political, but also progressively takes over the whole of his being and leads to a general attitude of surrender....

At the same time, this crystallization closes his mind to all new ideas. The individual now has a set of prejudices and beliefs.... His entire personality now revolves around those elements. Every new idea will therefore be troublesome to his entire being."

In *Comments on the Society of the Spectacle*, Guy DeBord summed up the primary function of the mainstream media, "For what is communicated are orders; and with perfect harmony, those who give them are also those who tell us what they think of them."

For a deeper understanding, let's return to Ellul:

"Governmental propaganda suggests that public opinion demand this or that decision; it provokes the will of the people, who spontaneously say nothing. But, once evoked, formed, and crystallized on a point, that *will* becomes the *people's will*.

The government really acts on its own, it just gives the impression of obeying public opinion, after having first built that public opinion. The point is to make the masses demand of the government what the government has already decided to do."

They "amputate the argument" and replace it with "engineered consensus." As Robert Lynd wrote in *Democracy In Reverse*, "They operate actually to confirm the citizen's false sense of security in totaling up 'what the majority think'... The false sense of the public's being 'boss' that they encourage operates to narcotize public awareness of the seriousness of problems and of the drastic social changes many contemporary situations require."

James Madison also realized this when he wrote, "The larger a country, the less easy for its real opinion to be ascertained, and the less difficult to be counterfeited." That was written in 1791, when the US population was only about five million people. Bertrand Russell also hit at the root in *Free Thought and Official Propaganda*, when he said, "it is much easier than it used to be to spread misinformation, and, owing to democracy, the spread of misinformation is more important than in former times to the holders of power."

Once the mainstream media has created the impression that public opinion is in favor of something, people are much more inclined to support that opinion themselves. In 1935, Malcolm Willey explained, "An individual may be moved to action through repetition, as, for example, in advertising; but his action is made more certain if he is made to realize that thousands, even millions, of others are thinking and feeling as he himself does. Herein lies the importance of the contemporary communication network; it not only carries its symbols to the individual, it also impresses upon him a sense of numbers."

As social psychologist Gabriel Tarde wrote in 1901, "Newspapers have transformed... the conversations of individuals, even those who do not read papers but who, talking to those who do, are forced to follow the groove of their borrowed thoughts. One pen suffices to set off a million tongues."

In summation, as the .01% knows very well, if you have enough wealth to own mainstream media companies, you can limit and focus debate in terms that are favorable to your interests, and you can repetitiously condition the masses with messages and opinions that support your objectives.

In *Taking the Risk Out of Democracy*, Alex Carey summed it up in one sentence: "That this simple regime of thought-control should prove to have been so triumphant, with so little public resistance, must be put down to its persistent, repetitive orchestration."

Chapter 9
Indoctrinated Intelligentsia

"Circus dogs jump when the trainer cracks his whip,
but the really well-trained dog is the one that
turns his somersault when there is no whip."
~ George Orwell, As I Please

What the old masters used to do with whips, they now do with paychecks. The .01% conditions the population through the mainstream media and they use their wealth to coerce, bribe and indoctrinate the administrative class into propagating their ideology. An indoctrinated intelligentsia has been produced like products off an assembly line. In *The Genesis of the Technocratic Elite*, Zoran Vidakovic breaks down how the assembly line of indoctrination works:

"Selection, education, and specific indoctrination of technical and administrative cadres are carried out first in metropolitan educational and research factories and their branches in dependent societies, under the wing of the superficially independent foundations which sustain the international projects of 'technical aid,' and then within the personnel policy of the transnational corporations that raise people from the local environments to responsible managerial and technical functions in their internationally located branches, or that in other ways subordinate and direct the 'modernized' industrial entrepreneurs, agrarian 'reformers,' functionaries, and leading intellectuals from the ministries and banks, universities, and public information, cultural, and scientific institutions.

The essential effect of this great factory for the almost assembly line production of dependent and emasculated 'technocratic elites' is that the material position, status, and professional success of the members of these groups imperatively depends on their conformity to the ideology of dependence and the interiorization of the intellectual, political, and ideological characteristics of this social type programmed in metropolitan laboratories for the technological, social, and cultural transformation of 'developing countries.'...

The ideology of total repression unites with the ideology of technological and cultural dependency and assimilation; in this union repression gains strength as the condition of the entire dependent economic growth, technological progress, and 'modernization of society,' as a circle of insurmountable dependency on the import of prefabricated knowledge and technical and consumerist models is closed up by the ambitions of the protagonists of authoritarian rule."

As you can see, you don't need a conspiracy theory to understand this system of indoctrination and mental conditioning; you just need to have a basic understanding of social psychology and behaviorism. We live in a Skinner box. It's classic "behavioral modification" (b-mod) within a "token economy." The .01% incentivizes and rewards certain behavior, and they punish or withdraw basic necessities for other behavior.

It's behaviorism 101. Give people a paycheck to have certain opinions and do certain things. You can see it everywhere, in almost all professions, not just the media. If you think a certain way, if you do certain things, you will be awarded with a paycheck. If you don't, you lose your paycheck. Or, to paraphrase Thomas Paine in *Rights of Man*, 'Those who do not participate in this enacting do not get fed.'

As W.E.H. Lecky once said, 'The simple fact of applying certain penalties to the profession of particular opinions, and rewards to the profession of opposite opinions, while it will make many hypocrites, it will also make many converts.'

If you propagate the message of the .01% and uphold the status quo, you can become rich and famous. That's what shortsighted ego-driven careerists do. They are the ultimate pawns of empire. They enrich themselves by riding the coattails of conquerors.

The bottom line is the bottom line; you either bow down and play by their rules or you lose access to basic necessities. It's the root of modern monetary and mental enslavement.

The Economics of Revolution

Chapter 10
Free Your Mind ~*~

"You have to understand, most of these people are not ready to be unplugged. And many of them are so inured, so hopelessly dependent on the system, that they will fight to protect it... Sooner or later you're going to realize, just as I did, that there's a difference between knowing the path, and walking the path. I'm trying to free your mind... But I can only show you the door.
You're the one that has to walk through it."
~ *The Matrix*

When you expose mental conditioning processes, the false reality and illusions that people are trapped in, the propagandized mind will instinctively dismiss or attack you. When it comes to the reactionary propagandized mind, their impulsive, instinctive dismissal further demonstrates how well they have been indoctrinated and conditioned. People will bite your hand when you try to remove the mental leash from their neck.

As Mihaly Csikszentmihalyi explained in *The Evolving Self*, "To prevent its annihilation, the ego forces us to be constantly on the watch for anything that might threaten the symbols on which it relies for identity. Our view of the world becomes polarized into 'good' and 'bad' – things that support the image, and those that threaten it." This is also how the third Mayan veil works. In this case, our media created cultural programming; it distorts reality to make it congruent with conditioned views.

Anything that deviates from the conditioned norm is ridiculed and instantly, instinctively dismissed before critical thinking skills are activated. The repetitious conditioning process leads to an *amputation of critical thinking faculties*. That which people are not familiar with becomes evil and damaging to their mental construct, to their conditioned thought patterns and their fabricated self-image.

We tend to look for anything that confirms our pre-existing beliefs while ignoring anything that goes against them. This is how confirmation bias works, to paraphrase Bertrand Russell: 'If people are offered a fact which goes against their conditioning or cultural programming, they will refuse to believe it. If, on the other hand, they are offered something which goes in accordance to their conditioning, they will accept it, even on the slightest evidence.'

Carl Sagan referred to this as being in a state of bamboozlement: "One of the saddest lessons of history is this: If we've been bamboozled long enough, we tend to reject any evidence of the bamboozle. We're no longer interested in finding out the truth. The bamboozle has captured us. It's simply too painful to acknowledge, even to ourselves, that we've been taken. Once you give a charlatan power over you, you almost never get it back."

Until you see the walls, you can't break free. As Aldous Huxley put it in *Brave New World Revisited*, "The victim of mind-manipulation does not know that they are a victim. To them, the walls of their prison are invisible, and they believe they are free." When it comes to the current mental conditioning process, *it's hard to break free when you are repetitively told you are free.*

Having been bred within this all-pervasive propaganda system, I understand the disbelief people feel. When our conditioned belief system is called into question and comes crashing down, it is a hard pill to swallow. No one wants to believe that they have been manipulated or taken advantage of. This will stir up an instinctive dismissal, a powerful emotional response. We are creatures of habit, and it is much easier, over the *short-term*, to just stay on a path of denial and ignorance. Hear no evil. See no evil.

Toward Freedom

The task is to consciously counter conditioned consciousness. The most difficult and important prerequisite to freedom is the ability to see past all of your culturally programmed biases. It takes great personal inner-strength and determination to achieve this. You will inevitably have to face many facts that will go against your programmed, conditioned beliefs. If you can endure this, you will experience true freedom.

As Mihaly Csikszentmihalyi put it in *The Evolving Self*, "In order to gain control of consciousness, we must learn how to moderate the biases built into the machinery of the brain. We allow a whole series of illusions to stand between ourselves and reality.... These distortions are comforting, yet they need to be seen through for the self to be truly liberated... to come ever closer to getting a glimpse of the universal order, and of our part in it."

Even if a person is strong enough to have an awareness of their conditioning, it is another level to confront and transcend it. As Nietzsche said in *Twilight of the Idols*, "Even the most courageous among us only rarely has the courage for that which he really knows."

> "Are you brave enough to see?
> Do you want to change it?"
> ~ Trent Reznor, The Hand That Feeds

Noam Chomsky makes the ease in which you can free your mind clear, and stresses the importance of doing so:

> "To take apart the system of illusions and deception which functions to prevent understanding of contemporary reality is not a task that requires extraordinary skill or understanding. It requires the kind of normal skepticism and willingness to apply one's analytical skills that almost all people have and that they can exercise....
>
> As long as some specialized class is in position of authority, it is going to set policy in the special interests that it serves, but the conditions of survival, let alone justice, require rational social planning in the interests of the community as a whole, and by now that means the global community.
>
> The question is whether privileged elite should dominate mass communication and should use this power as they tell us they must – namely to impose necessary illusions, to manipulate and deceive.... In this possibly terminal phase of human existence, democracy and freedom are more than values to be treasured; they may well be essential to survival."

Most of us are aware that our economic and political systems are overrun with corruption and that society is on a disastrous path. However, many of us feel powerless to change things. It is stunning to hear so many people say that they can't do anything about it. Far too many people think that we can't create change; that is the primary reason why we don't. Why do you think that we can't change the world? How did you come to that conclusion? Who taught you to believe that?

These beliefs are only a result of our conditioning; it's a propaganda-induced delusion. We have become so propagandized that many of us do not realize the significant position that we are in. We are a critical mass of people who have the power to evolve society and change the course of history.

The *overwhelming* majority feels powerless to create political change. If they would just realize that they are the *overwhelming* majority, they would no longer feel this way. As Ellul said, "Only when he realizes his delusion will he experience the beginning of genuine freedom – in the act of realization itself – be it only from the effort to stand back and look squarely at the phenomenon and reduce it to raw fact."

As Malcolm X said, "I say and I say it again, you've been had. You've been took. You've been hoodwinked, bamboozled, led astray, run amok." We live in the richest and most technologically advanced society in the history of civilization. There is no reason for poverty to exist. People should not have to struggle and be buried in debt to get basic necessities and live a healthy life. We've been hoodwinked, bamboozled and led astray, as the .01% runs amok.

Transcend Conditioned Consciousness

Time comes and times go...

Thanks to the Internet, people are now freeing their minds from conditioning. The Internet is to our generation what pamphlets were to our forefathers' during the first American Revolution. People are using the Internet to find out all the vital information that the mainstream media is not letting people know about. As a result, we now have a critical mass of informed and outraged citizens.

As William Adams Brown said, "We are developing a social conscience, and situations which would have been accepted a generation ago as a matter of course are felt as an intolerable scandal." John Dewey continues, "Liberty in the concrete signifies release from the impact of particular oppressive forces; emancipation from something once taken as a normal part of human life but now experienced as bondage.... Today, it signifies liberation from material insecurity and from the coercions and repressions that prevent multitudes from participation in the vast cultural resources that are at hand."

The inevitable demise of the .01% was summed up by George Orwell when he said, "For if leisure and security were enjoyed by all alike, the great mass of human beings who are normally stupefied by poverty would become literate and would learn to think for themselves; and when once they had done this, they would sooner or later realize that the privileged minority had no function, and they would sweep it away. In the long run, a hierarchical society was only possible on a basis of poverty and ignorance."

As Thomas Jefferson once said, "Enlighten the people generally, and tyranny and oppressions of body and mind will vanish like evil spirits at the dawn of day."

People are throwing off their mental shackles and realizing their potential. We are now transcending conditioned consciousness and expanding our awareness on a scale unprecedented in human history. An empowering consciousness is evolving.

Emancipate Yourself From Mental Slavery
NONE BUT OURSELVES CAN FREE OUR MINDS
Transcend Conditioned Consciousness
BREAK ON THROUGH...

PART III

NOW IS THE TIME

The Economics of Revolution

Chapter 11
A Critical Crossroad

A new paradigm is organically evolving: new economic systems, sustainable communities, solar energy, organic farming, liquid democracy, worker co-ops and new media. For all the problems we are confronted by, there are existing viable solutions. There is much to feel positive about. A decentralized global uprising is undermining systems of centralized and consolidated power. A new world is being born.

However, as exciting as the evolution presently occurring is, after extensive research I am forced to confront the fact that I do not see how emerging solutions will reach a critical mass and create the needed change before the effects of poverty and the overall deterioration of society will lead to chaos and violence on a mass scale.

As much as I wish this wasn't the case, as much as I want to just disengage from the status quo and focus on the implementation of local solutions, we cannot ignore the urgent need for *significant systemic change* on a mass scale *now*.

The longer mainstream society stays on the present course, the worse things will get and the harder it will be to overcome the growing crisis. No matter how much we are inclined to ignore it, will we not be able to escape this reality: under present economic and government policy, more and more people will fall deeper into debt and poverty. A quickly growing number of people cannot afford basic necessities. Tens of millions of people are being thrown overboard. Mainstream propaganda has temporarily obscured the fact that we are sitting on a ticking economic time bomb.

Just when the economy has reached a point where there are not enough jobs that generate an adequate income to sustain the cost of living *for the majority of the population*, the government is cutting billions of dollars from assistance programs and pouring billions of dollars into the military and prison industry.

An out of control private military complex is fueling violent conflicts abroad. Here at home, the police force is being militarized and the private prison industry is growing at a shocking 1600% rate. We already have the largest prison population in the world. The current per capita rate is worse than the darkest days of the Soviet Gulags. Many cities are now criminalizing poverty. A tyrannical assembly line of incarceration is in place.

Based on existing evidence and key indicators, it is logical to think that increased desperation within large segments of the population will soon lead to chaos and riots. Also factor in the militarized police force, which will escalate violence and oppression. This scenario is highly probable, and it will tear our nation apart.

We are at a critical crossroad.

Are we on the verge of an evolutionary leap, or will shortsighted greed descend us into madness and destruction?

Will significant systemic change happen quick enough to prevent a much larger collapse?

The ultimate point is that *there is presently more than enough wealth and capabilities to solve societal problems.* We can truly evolve society in unprecedented fashion. A significant portion of the population and even many of the ultra-rich realize that our present system is obsolete, unsustainable and unstable. We already have a critical mass of aware citizens, we just need to inspire and organize them to build the *cultural and political will.*

If we want to change things through nonviolent methods, the window of opportunity is closing fast. We need to radically intensify the pace in which change is occurring. The .01% and political class must urgently acquiesce to the needs of the people. As John Kennedy once said, "Those who make peaceful revolution impossible will make violent revolution inevitable."

The statistical evidence is clear.

We have reached *the tipping point.*

Revolution is coming, one way or the other.

The Economics of Revolution

70